Learn & Color Nature Series
Medicinal Herbs

LEARN AND COLOR

Fulton, KY

Subscribe and Save

We offer a new way for you to receive more and more coloring books at a significant savings through our subscription option.

Each month your next coloring book can be delivered right to your mail box. You'll receive a discount from the retail price with shipping and handling included!

Find out all the details and sign up today
http://LearnAndColor.com/educational

Learn and Color Nature Series – Medicinal Herbs
© 2018 Master Design Marketing, LLC

All rights reserved. This book or parts thereof may not be reproduced in any form, stored in any retrieval system, or transmitted in any form by any means—electronic, mechanical, photocopy, recording, or otherwise—without prior written permission of the publisher, except as provided by United States of America copyright law. For permission requests, write to the publisher, at "Attention: Permissions Coordinator," at the address below.

Learn & Color Books
 an imprint of Master Design Marketing, LLC
 789 State Route 94 E
 Fulton, KY 42041
 www.LearnAndColor.com

For information about special discounts available for bulk purchases, sales promotions, fund-raising and educational needs, contact Learn & Color Books Company Sales at sales@LearnAndColor.com.

ISBN: 978-1-947482-07-4

Important. Please Read: This book is for the presentation of the historical uses of herbs and its contents are for informational purposes only. Never take any herb or health supplement without first consulting your doctor. Never take any herb or supplement without your doctor's consent if you are pregnant, nursing, or trying to get pregnant. Never give herbs or health supplements to children without first talking to their doctor. The statements made in this book have not been evaluated by the FDA. The herbs and supplements mentioned are not intended to cure, treat, diagnose or prevent disease. Always play it safe.

Cover design by Faithe F Thomas
Photos and Illustrations © 123RF
Text in this book is a derivative of information by Wikipedia.com, used under CC BY 4.0.
The text of this book is licensed under CC BY 4.0 by Faithe F Thomas.
Look for the Scottish Flag somewhere in each of our books.

Sample Pages from
Learn & Color Nature Series – Medicinal Herbs

American Ginseng

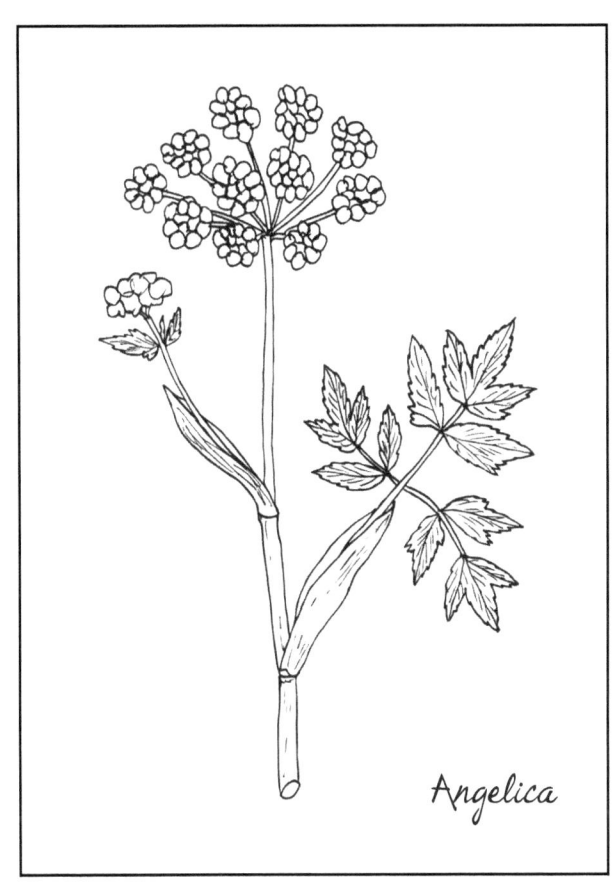

Angelica

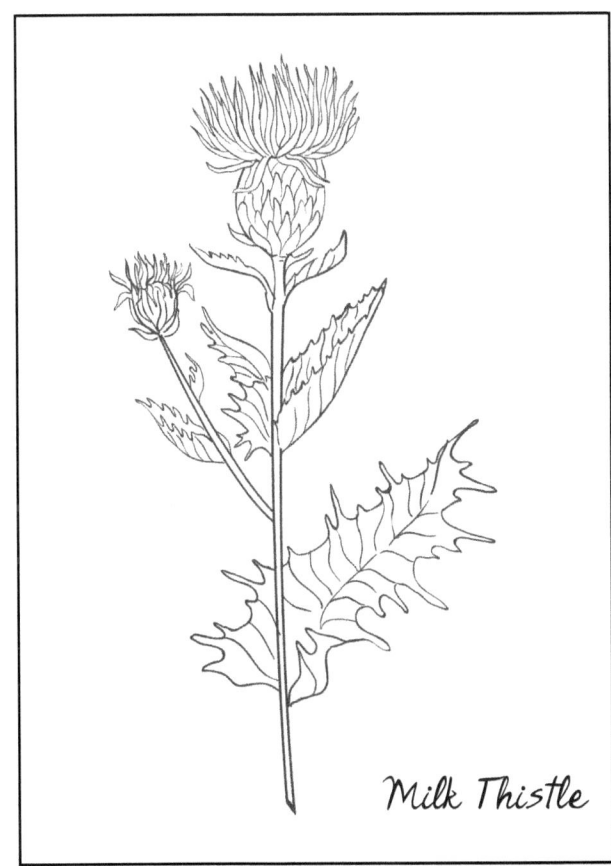

Milk Thistle

St. John's Wort

Alfalfa
Medicago sativa

Important Facts

- Called the "Father of all foods"
- Loaded with important vitamins, minerals, trace minerals and protein.
- Used for arthritis, digestive problems, as a diuretic and for reducing high cholesterol.
- High in beta-carotene and builds the immune system.
- Contains chlorophyll, good for reducing bad breath and body odor.

Common Names
Buffalo grass, chilean clover, lucerne

Parts Used
Leaves, stems, sprouts

Habitat
Alfalfa is native to southwestern Asia and SE Europe. Also grows in North America and North Africa.

Cautions
Never eat alfalfa seeds.

Other Information
Alfalfa is a perennial flowering plant in the legume family Fabaceae. The name alfalfa is used in North America. The name lucerne is the more commonly used name in the United Kingdom, South Africa, Australia, and New Zealand.

Aloe

Aloe
Aloe vera

Important Facts

- Gel inside of the leaves are used externally to treat minor burns, sun burn, cuts, scrapes and poison ivy.
- A good skin moisturizer and is often a main ingredient of many skin care products.
- Many people use it to reduce acne and treat other skin problems.

Common Names
Aloe, cape, barbados

Parts Used
Leaves

Habitat
Aloe is native to the Mediterranean. It also grows in Latin America and the Caribbean

Cautions
The Mayo Clinic website states that it is not safe to use Aloe internally and can lead to severe cramping, diarrhea, and dangerous imbalances of electrolytes even if used infrequently.

Other Information
Aloe vera is a succulent plant species of the genus Aloe. An evergreen perennial, it is cultivated for agricultural, medicinal uses, and decorative purposes. Aloe grows successfully indoors as a potted plant.

American Ginseng
Panax quinquefolius

Important Facts
- Is good for the body in general and protects against stress of all types
- Strengthens the immune system, increases strength and stamina
- Treats digestive disorders, diabetes, ADHD, and a general tonic for wellness

Common Names
Ginseng, xi yang shen

Parts Used
Root

Habitat
American Ginseng grows in the eastern part of North America.

Cautions
- Should not be taken by people with high blood pressure
- Should not be taken by women who are pregnant.

Other Information
American ginseng is a herbaceous perennial plant in the ivy family, commonly used in Chinese or traditional medicine. Since the 18th century, American ginseng has been primarily exported to Asia, where it is highly valued for perceived superior quality and sweet taste.

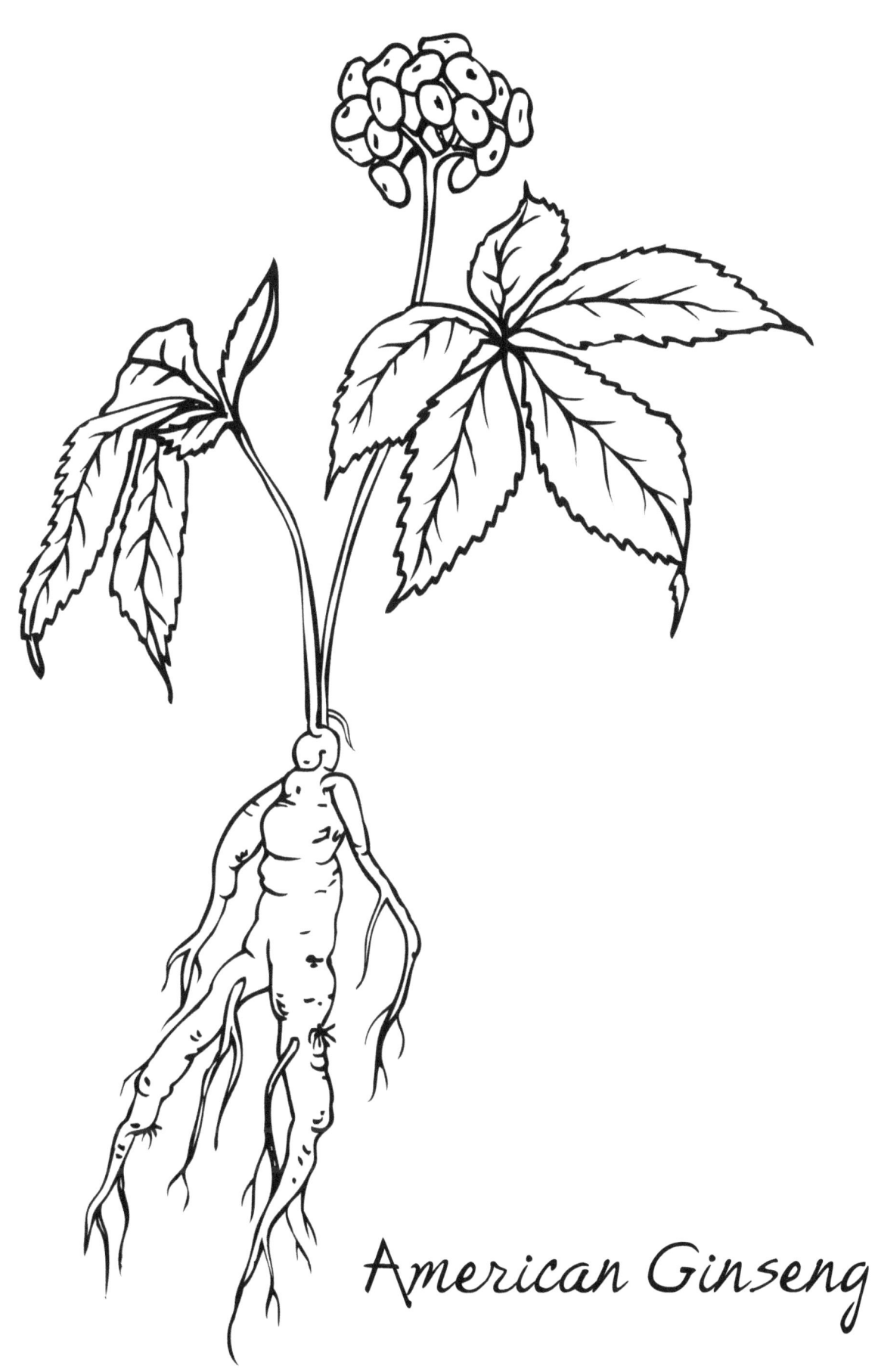

Angelica
Angelica archangelica

Important Facts

- Traditionally been used for menopausal troubles, flatulence, appetite loss, digestive problems, respiratory ailments, and arthritis.
- Not the same as its Chinese counterpart Angelica sinensis (dong quai)
- Used by many women for the reproductive system
- Believed to be a hormonal regulator and uterine tonic
- Angelica tea is often used to treat PMS.

Common Names
Garden angelica, norwegian angelica, holy ghost, wild celery

Parts Used
Leaves, stems, seeds, roots

Habitat
Angelica grows in Asia, Europe and the eastern U.S

Cautions
Angelica is not recommended during pregnancy.

Other Information
Its appearance is similar to several poisonous species, and should not be consumed unless it has been identified with absolute certainty.

A flute-like instrument with a clarinet-like sound can be made of its hollow stem.

Anise
Illicium verum

Important Facts

- Anise tea is made from the plant's seeds.
- Has a strong licorice taste
- Star anise oil is a highly fragrant oil used in cooking, perfumery, soaps, toothpastes, mouthwashes, and skin creams.
- Not to be confused with Pimpinella anisum, the anise or aniseed used for flavor and some medicines, which is native to the Mediterranean region. Pimpinella anisum is said to improve digestion, prevent flatulence, reduce bad breath and treat coughs.

Common Names
Anise, Star Anise

Parts Used
Seeds

Habitat
Native to northeast Vietnam and southwest China

Cautions
Angelica is not recommended during pregnancy.

Other Information
Illicium verum is a medium-sized evergreen tree. About 90% of the world's star anise crop is used for extraction of shikimic acid, a chemical intermediate used in the synthesis of oseltamivir (Tamiflu).

Anise

Arnica

Arnica
Arnica montana

Important Facts
- Used externally as an ointment for sore muscles, sprains and bruises.
- Arnica montana is used as an herbal medicine for analgesic and anti-inflammatory purposes
- When used topically in a gel at 50% concentration, A. montana was found to have the same effectiveness as a 5% ibuprofen gel for treating the symptoms of hand osteoarthritis.

Common Names
Leopard's bane, mountain daisy, mountain arnica

Parts Used
Flowers

Habitat
Arnica is native to central Asia, Siberia and Europe. Cultivated in North America.

Cautions
Should never be taken internally.

Other Information
Arnica is a genus of perennial, herbaceous plants in the sunflower family. The demand for Arica is high, but the supply does not cover the demand. The plant is rare; it is protected in Belgium, France, Germany, Italy, Poland, and in some regions of Switzerland.

Bearberry
Arctostaphylos uva-ursi

Important Facts

- Makes a delicious tea.
- Used to treat urinary tract infections and inflammation of the urinary tract.
- Has astringent, diuretic and antiseptic properties.
- Bearberry is the main component in many traditional North American Native smoking mixes, known collectively as "kinnikinnick" (Algonquin for a mixture).

Common Names
Uva ursi, mountain box, bear's grape, kinnikinnick

Parts Used
Leaves

Habitat
Bearberry grows throughout the Northern Hemisphere

Cautions
Can be toxic in high doses. Never take it if you are pregnant or if you have kidney disease. Do not give Bearberry to children.

Other Information
Arctostaphylos uva-ursi is a small procumbent woody groundcover shrub 2-12 in high. The leaves are evergreen, remaining green for 1-3 years before falling. The fruit is a red berry.

Bearberry

Bee Balm

Bee Balm
Monarda didyma

Important Facts

- Used by the Native Americans to treat many problems, including intestinal problems, colic, and flatulence.
- Often used to treat the common cold and sore throat.
- Its oil is an antibiotic and often used as an ingredient in mouthwash.
- Its odor is considered similar to that of the bergamot orange (the source of bergamot oil used to flavor Earl Grey tea)

Common Names

Wswego tea, mountain mint, scarlet bergamot

Parts Used

Leaves

Habitat

Bee Balm is native to North America

Cautions

None known

Other Information

This hardy perennial plant grows to 2-4 feet in height. Crimson beebalm is extensively grown as an ornamental plant, both within and outside its native range. An herbal tea made from the plant was also used to treat mouth and throat infections caused by dental caries and gingivitis.

Bilberry
Vaccinium mytillus

Important Facts
- Used for centuries by European healers to treat such things as stomach cramps, diarrhea, and diabetes.
- Most often used to prevent night blindness.
- Contains flavonoids called anthocyanosides — a powerful antioxidant.
- Has also been used as a remedy for varicose veins, hemorrhoids, and bruising.

Common Names
European blueberry, huckleberry, whortleberry

Parts Used
Leaves, fruit

Habitat
Bilberry grows in the warm regions of the Northern Hemisphere

Cautions
None known

Other Information
European Bilberries are different from North American blueberries, although the species are closely related and belong to the same genus, Vaccinium. Bilberry are non-climacteric fruits with a smooth, circular outline at the end opposite the stalk, whereas blueberries retain persistent sepals there, leaving a rough, star-shaped pattern of five flaps.

These are bilberries...

These are blueberries!

Borage
Borago officinalis

Important Facts

- Used to treat fever, lung infections, inflammation of mucous membranes, and as a diuretic.
- May also be effective as a mild anti-depressant and sedative.
- an annual herb in the flowering plant family Boraginaceae

Common Names

Burrage, beebread, star flower, bee Plant, talewort

Parts Used

Flowers, seed oil

Habitat

Borage is native to Southern Europe

Cautions

None known

Other Information

Borage is used as either a fresh vegetable or a dried herb. As a fresh vegetable, borage, with a cucumber-like taste, is often used in salads or as a garnish. The flower has a sweet honey-like taste and is often used to decorate desserts and cocktails.

Burdock
Arctium Lappa

Important Facts

- Used by the ancient Greeks to treat wounds and infections
- Used to treat liver and digestive problems, urinary tract infections, ulcers, eczema, psoriasis, and to boost energy and stamina.
- Has anti-fungal and anti-bacterial properties and makes a good immune system booster and blood purifier.
- Plants of the genus Arctium have dark green leaves that can grow up to 28 in long

Common Names
Wild Burdock, gobo, burr, beggar's buttons

Parts Used
Seeds, leaves, and roots

Habitat
Burdock grows in the United States, Europe, Japan and China

Cautions
A strong detoxifier and could aggravate certain types of skin conditions before the healing process starts working. May interfere with several prescription drugs, like those for treating diabetes or blood sugar conditions. Pregnant or nursing women should talk with their doctor before taking this herb.

Other Information
Dandelion and burdock is today a soft drink that has long been popular in the United Kingdom, which has its origins in hedgerow mead commonly drunk in the mediæval period.

Burdock

Calendula
Calendula officinalis

Important Facts

- Has been used to induce menstruation, break fevers, cure jaundice, treat open sores, and for liver and stomach problems.
- Has antiseptic and anti-inflammatory properties.
- Can even be used externally for sunburn and eczema.
- Used externally to treat slow healing wounds and to promote tissue repair.

Common Names
Pot marigold, poet's mairgold, Cape Weed

Parts Used
Flowers

Habitat
Calendula is native to the Mediterranean region

Cautions
Do not take Calendula internally if pregnant or nursing. Could cause miscarriage.

Other Information
Calendula is a genus of about 15-20 species of annual and perennial herbaceous plants in the daisy family Asteraceae that are often known as marigolds. The petals are edible and can be used fresh in salads or dried and used to color cheese or as a replacement for saffron.

Catnip
Nepeta cataria

Important Facts

- Used to treat coughs, scalp irritations, bruises, restlessness, and gas.
- Used to treat upset stomach, colic, colds, fever, flu, and diarrhea.
- Sometimes used to treat inflammation, allergies, and as a mild sedative.
- Nepeta cataria is a short-lived perennial, herbaceous plant that grows to be 20-39 inches tall and wide, which blooms from late-spring to the autumn.

Common Names

Catmint, catswort, catnep, catrup

Parts Used

Flowers, Leaves

Habitat

Catnip is native to Asia and Europe

Cautions

- Do not take if you are pregnant or nursing, as it may stimulate the uterus and cause miscarriage.
- Do not give to children.
- Unsafe to smoke.

Other Information

Nepetalactone is a mosquito and fly repellent. Oil isolated from catnip by steam distillation is a repellent against insects, in particular mosquitoes, cockroaches and termites. Research suggests that, while ten times more effective than DEET, it is not as effective as a repellent when used on the skin when compared with SS220.

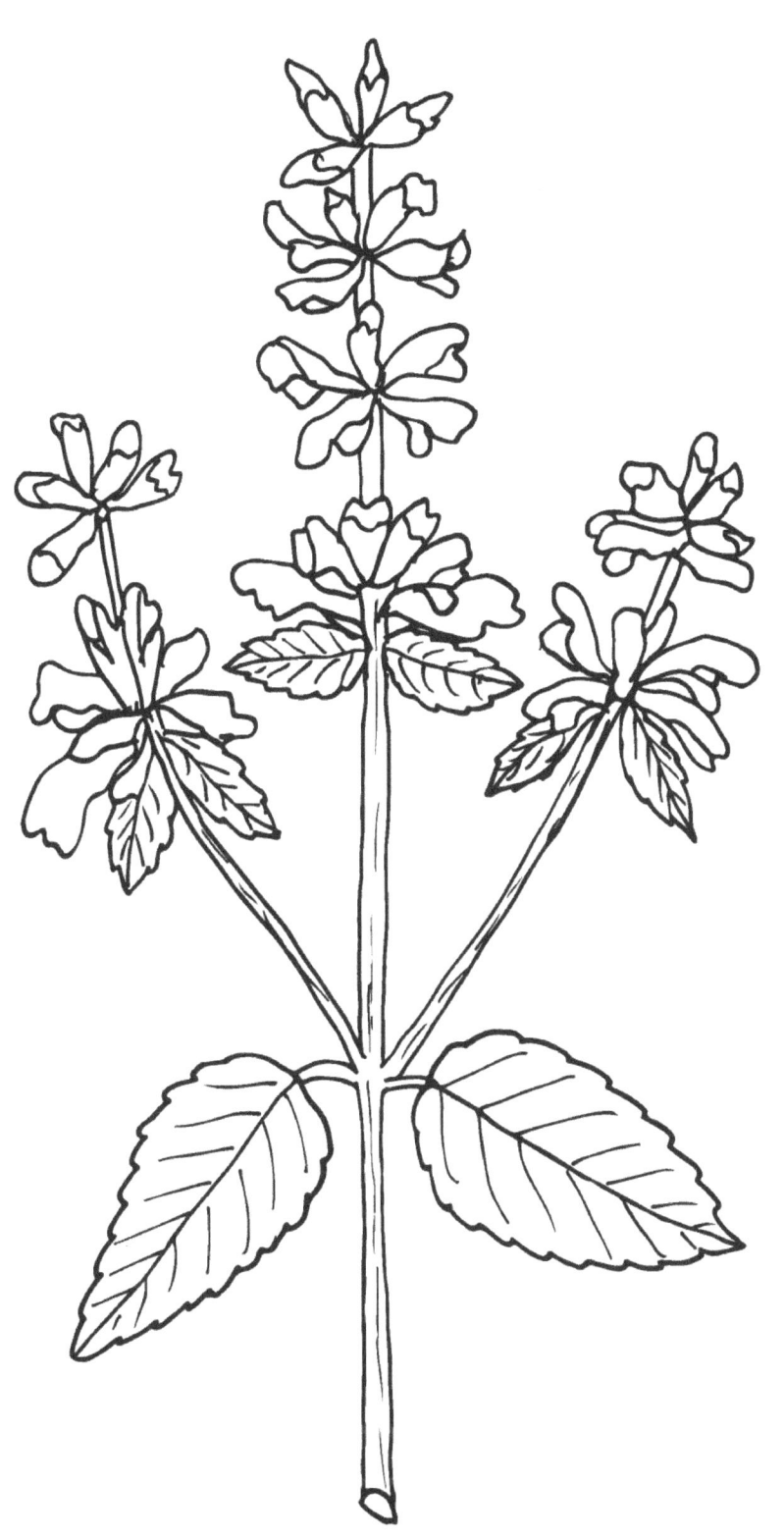

Catnip

Cayenne
Capsicum annuum

Important Facts

- Used by Native Americans as a pain reliever and to halt infections.
- Used for toothaches, arthritiss and to aid digestion.
- Has anti-bacterial properties, can stimulate blood flows and is rich in vitamins, mineralss and antioxidants.
- May reduce triglyceride levels and platelet aggregation in the blood.

Common Names
Red pepper, capsicum, chili pepper

Parts Used
Fruit

Habitat
Cayenne is native to tropical regions of the Americas

Cautions
- May irritate the skin. Use care when handling.
- May cause stomach discomfort.

Other Information
Cayenne peppers are a group of tapering, 10 to 25 cm long, generally skinny, mostly red colored peppers, often with a curved tip and somewhat rippled skin, which hang from the bush as opposed to growing upright.

Chamomile
Matricaria recutita

Important Facts

- Has been used for fever and chills
- Used for colic, indigestion, flatulence, bloating, heartburn, and to calm nervousness.
- Has anti-inflammatory, antifungal, antiseptic, antibacterial and antispasmodic properties.
- The word "chamomile" derives, via French and Latin, from Greek (khamaimelon), i.e. "earth apple", from χαμαι (khamai) "on the ground" and μηλον (melon) "apple". The more common British spelling "camomile," is the older one in English, while the spelling "chamomile" corresponds to the Latin and Greek source. The spelling camomile is a derivation from the French.

Common Names

German chamomile, wild chamomile

Parts Used

Flower heads, oil

Habitat

Chamomile is native to Asia, Africa and Europe

Cautions

- May cause allergic reactions in people sensitive to ragweed or other plants in the daisy family.

Other Information

In The Tale of Peter Rabbit by Beatrix Potter (in 1902), the author refers to chamomile tea given to Peter after being chased by Mr. McGregor.

People who are allergic to ragweed (also in the daisy family) may be allergic to chamomile due to cross-reactivity.

Chicory
Cichorium intybus

Important Facts

- Often used by the Native Americans for cleaning the blood and diuretic.
- Used to treat loss of appetite and indigestion.
- Common chicory is a somewhat woody, perennial herbaceous plant of the dandelion family Asteraceae, usually with bright blue flowers, rarely white or pink.

Common Names

Succory, wild succory, coffeeweed

Parts Used

Whole herb

Habitat

Chicory is native to Asia, Europe and North America

Cautions

- People with gallstones should not consume chicory.

Other Information

Root chicory has been cultivated in Europe as a coffee substitute. It has been more widely used during economic crises such as the Great Depression in the 1930s and during World War II in Continental Europe as well as in prisons.

It is used as a sweetener in the food industry with a sweetening power 1/10 that of sucrose and is sometimes added to yogurts as a prebiotic.

Comfrey
Symphytum officinale

Important Facts

- Used as a poultice by the ancient Greeks to stop bleeding.
- Comfrey (Symphytum officinale L.) is a perennial herb of the family Boraginaceae with a black, turnip-like root and large, hairy broad leaves that bears small bell-shaped flowers of various colours, typically cream or purplish, which may be striped.
- Comfrey is a source of fertilizer to the organic gardener.

Common Names

Knitbone, slippery root, blackwort

Parts Used

Leaves, roots

Habitat

Comfrey is native to Europe and Asia

Cautions

Never take comfrey internally. It has recently been shown to cause severe liver damage.

Other Information

Folk medicine names for comfrey include knitbone and boneset. Similarly the common French name is consoude, meaning to weld together. The tradition in different cultures and languages suggest a common belief in its usefulness for mending bones.

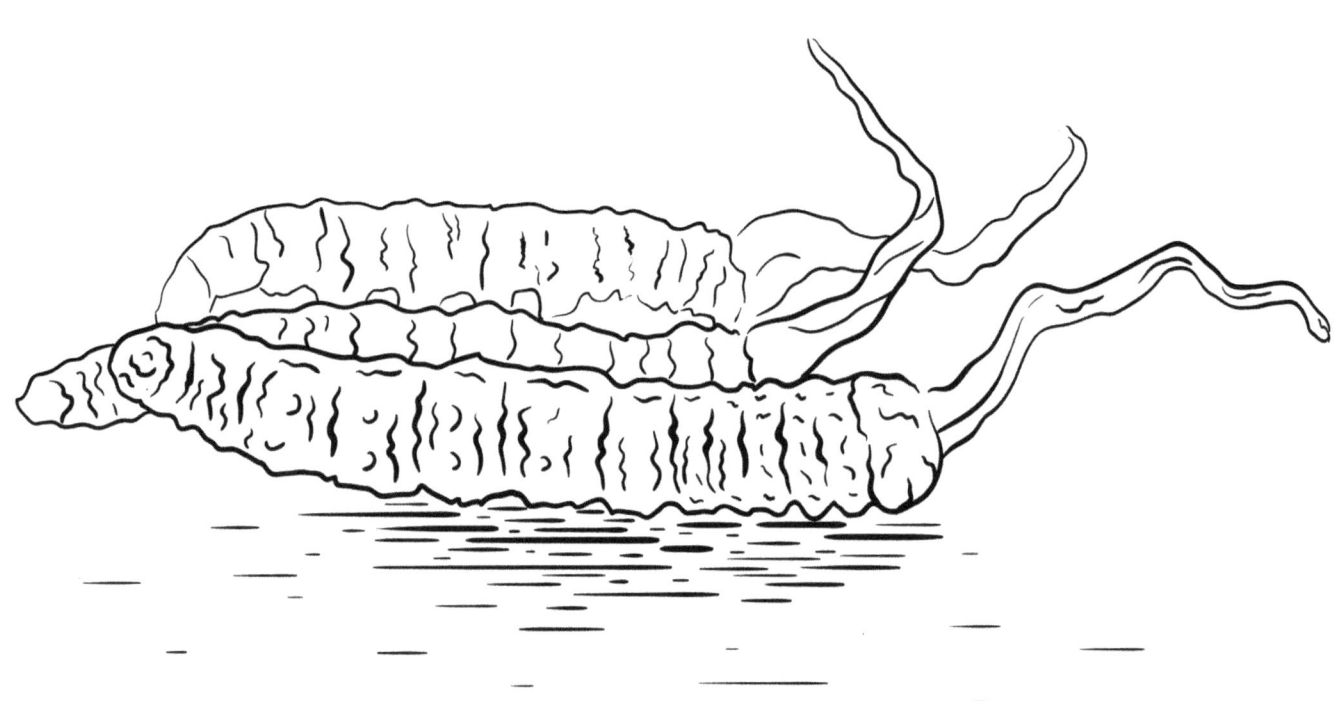

Cordyceps

Cordyceps

Cordyceps sinensis or Ophiocordyceps sinensis

Important Facts

- Considered a great tonic for building physical strength and endurance.
- Dilates the lung's airways, providing more oxygen to the blood.
- Used to treat asthma, cough, and bronchitis.
- Possesses anti-inflammatory properties and has the ability to relax the bronchial walls.
- A great immune system booster
- C. sinensis was shown in 2007 by nuclear DNA sampling to be unrelated to most of the rest of the members of the genus; as a result it was renamed Ophiocordyceps sinensis and placed in a new family, the Ophiocordycipitaceae, as was "Cordyceps unilateralis".

Common Names

Caterpillar fungus, Zhiling, Cs-4, yartsa gunbu

Parts Used

Fruiting body

Habitat

Cordyceps mushrooms grows wild on the Himalayan Plateau

Cautions

None

Other Information

In traditional Chinese medicine (TCM), it is regarded as having an excellent balance of yin and yang as it is considered to be composed of both an animal and a vegetable.

In rural Tibet, yartsa gunbu has become the most important source of cash income. The fungi contributed 40% of the annual cash income to local households and 8.5% to the GDP in 2004.

Dandelion
Taraxacum officinale

Important Facts

- Used as a potent diuretic and detoxifying herb.
- Used to treat breast inflammation, digestive disorders, appendicitis, and to stimulate milk flow.
- Used as a remedy for eye problems, diarrhea, diabetes, and fever.
- Many similar plants in the Asteraceae family with yellow flowers are sometimes known as false dandelions.

Common Names
Lion's tooth, blowball, fairy clock, wetweed, priests Crown

Parts Used
Leaves, flowers, root

Habitat
Dandelion is native to Europe and Asia but grow all over the world

Cautions
Dandelion pollen may cause allergic reactions when eaten.

Other Information
Dandelions have been used by humans for food and as an herb for much of recorded history. They were well known to ancient Egyptians, Greeks and Romans, and have been used in Chinese traditional medicine for over a thousand years. Dandelions probably arrived in North America on the Mayflower—not as stowaways, but brought on purpose for their medicinal benefits.

Echinacea
Echinacea purpurea

Important Facts

- Very popular for treating colds and flu.
- A great immune system booster.
- Enjoyed as a healthy tea.
- Used for sore throat and upper respiratory tract infections.
- A good detoxifier and has antiviral, anti-inflammatory and antibiotic properties.
- Echinacea purpurea is an herbaceous perennial up to 47 in tall by 10 in wide at maturity.
- Slugs eat this plant. Rabbits will also eat the foliage when young, or shortly after emerging in the spring.

Common Names
Purple coneflower, coneflower, purple encinacea

Parts Used
Roots, leaves and flowers

Habitat
Echinacea is native to Central and Eastern North America

Cautions
Side effects include gastrointestinal effects and allergic reactions, including rashes, increased asthma, and life-threatening anaphylaxis.

Other Information
In indigenous medicine of the native American Indians, the plant was used externally for wounds, burns, and insect bites, chewing of roots for toothache and throat infections; internal application was used for pain, cough, stomach cramps, and snake bites.

It is purported that all parts of the purple coneflower stimulate the immune system.

Ginkgo Biloba
Ginkgo biloba

Important Facts

- Improves the flow of blood to the brain and increases oxygen to the brain cells.
- Suggested as a cognitive enhancer and memory booster.
- Possesses anti-coagulating properties and prevents the formation of blood clots.
- Contains powerful antioxidants.
- is the only living species in the division Ginkgophyta, all others being extinct. It is found in fossils.

Common Names

Ginkgo, bao gou, Yin-hsing, Maidenhair tree

Parts Used

Leaves and seeds

Habitat

Ginkgo biloba is native China but is also cultivated in Japan, France and the southern United States.

Cautions

- Can sometimes cause headaches and dizziness if taken in large doses.
- Never take ginkgo if you are taking anti-depressants such as MAOI or SRRI medicines.

Other Information

Ginkgos are large trees, normally reaching a height of 66–115 ft, with some specimens in China being over 160 ft. For centuries, it was thought to be extinct in the wild, but is now known to grow in at least two small areas in eastern China and southern Japan.

Ginkgo Biloba

Gotu Kola
Centella asiatica

Important Facts

- Used historically to relieve congestion from upper respiratory infections and colds and for wound healing.
- Used for treating varicose veins and memory loss.
- Grows in temperate and tropical swampy areas in many world regions.

Common Names

Centella, Indian pennywort, Brahmi, Luei gong gen

Parts Used

Leaves, Stems

Habitat

Gotu Kola grows in Africa, North and South America, Asia, Australia and Madagascar

Cautions

- The herb may have adverse effects on liver function when used over many months
- May cause sensitivity to sunlight and should never be taken by people with skin cancer.
- Contact dermatitis and skin irritation are possible from topical application

Other Information

In Myanmar cuisine, raw pennywort is used as the main constituent in a salad made also with onions, crushed peanuts, bean powder and seasoned with lime juice and fish sauce. Centella is used as a leafy green in Sri Lankan cuisine, being the most predominant of all locally available leafy greens, where it is called gotu kola.

Holy Basil
Ocimum Sanctum

Important Facts
- Used for reducing stress, anxiety and depression.
- Promotes health and wellbeing and protects the body and mind in a very positive way.
- Enhances cerebral circulation and improve memory.
- For centuries, the dried leaves have been mixed with stored grains to repel insects.

Common Names
Tulsi, Sacred basil, Surasa, Tulasi, Kemangen

Parts Used
Leaves, Stems

Habitat
Holy Basil is native to India

Cautions
- Has the ability to thin the blood and should not be taken along with blood thinning medications.
- Should not by taken by persons with hypoglycemia.
- Should never be taken by women trying to get pregnant. Never take if pregnant or nursing without first consulting your doctor.

Other Information
Tulasi is cultivated for religious and traditional medicine purposes, and for its essential oil. It is widely used as a herbal tea, commonly used in Ayurveda.

Lemongrass

Lemongrass
Cymbopogon citratus

Important Facts

- Used to treat cancer, stomach problems, nervous disorders, fevers, arthritis, flu, gas, pain, and others.
- Helps reduce anxiety and promotes sound sleep.
- Used externally, it can treat skin problems and keep the skin moist and clear.
- Research shows that lemongrass oil has antifungal properties.
- Despite its ability to repel some insects, such as mosquitoes, its oil is commonly used as a "lure" to attract honey bees.

Common Names

Silky heads, fever grass, barbed wire grass, tanglad, hierba Luisa, citronella grass or gavati chaha

Parts Used

Grass

Habitat

Lemongrass is native to tropical Asia and India

Cautions

- Should NOT be taken if pregnant since it has uterine stimulating properties.

Other Information

Lemongrass is widely used as a culinary herb in Asian cuisines and also as medicinal herb in India. It has a subtle citrus flavor and can be dried and powdered, or used fresh. It is commonly used in teas, soups, and curries. It is also suitable for use with poultry, fish, beef, and seafood.

Lycium Berry
Lycium barbarum

Important Facts

- One of the most nutritious foods on earth
- Eaten for their high antioxidant value
- The fruit has also been an ingredient in traditional Chinese, Korean, Vietnamese, and Japanese medicine, since at least the 3rd century
- Since the early 21st century, the dried fruit has been marketed in the Western world as a health food, amidst scientifically unsupported claims regarding such benefits.

Common Names

Goji, wolfberry

Parts Used

Fruit

Habitat

Lycium grows in Northwestern China and Tibet

Cautions

- Do not take if you have low blood pressure.
- Lycium can effect how quickly the liver breaks down some medications.

Other Information

In vitro testing suggests that unidentified wolfberry phytochemicals in goji tea may inhibit metabolism of other medications, such as those processed by the cytochrome P450 liver enzymes. Such drugs include warfarin, or drugs for diabetes or hypertension.

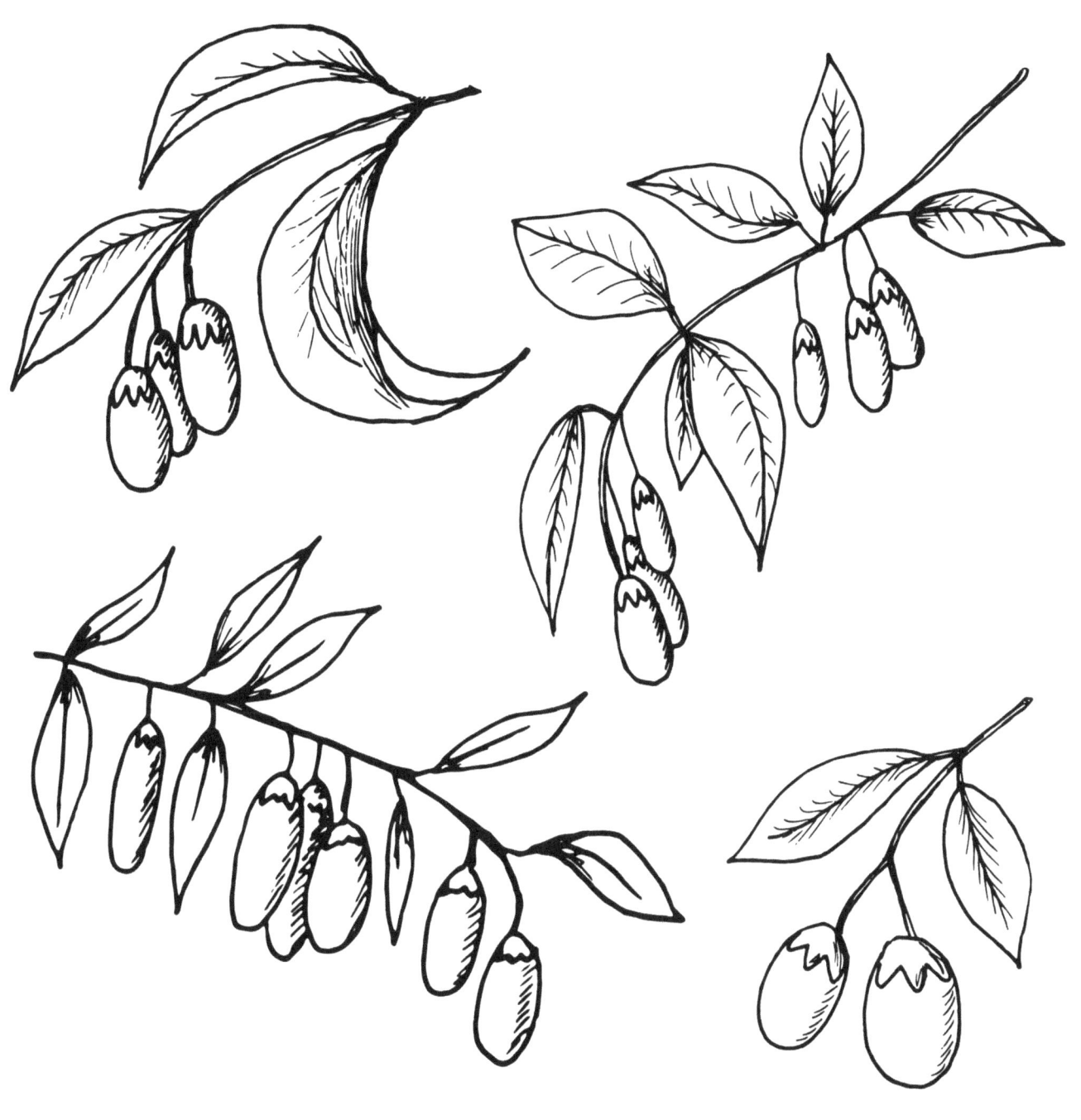

Lycium Berry

Maca

Maca
Lepidium meyenii

Important Facts

- Helps the body cope with stress
- Rich in vitamins, minerals, good fats, plant sterols, and amino acids
- Sometimes called a "superfood"
- A great overall energy booster and popular with athletes
- Mostly used for increasing energy and balancing the hormones

Common Names

Peruvian ginseng

Parts Used

Root

Habitat

Maca is native to Peru

Cautions

- Has a high iodine content and should not be consumed by people having thyroid disease
- Has stimulant properties and could possibly raise the heart rate
- May not be safe for pregnant women to use maca supplements

Other Information

There is archaeological evidence for varying degrees of cultivation of maca in the Lake Junin region from around 1700 BC to 1200 AD.

Milk Thistle
Silybum marianum

Important Facts
- A great protector of the liver and gallbladder
- Can detoxify the blood and is often taken to treat cancer
- This species is an annual or biennial plant of the Asteraceae family. This fairly typical thistle has red to purple flowers and shiny pale green leaves with white veins.

Common Names
Silymarin, Marian Thistle, Mediterranean Thistle, Mary Thistle

Parts Used
Seeds

Habitat
Milk Thistle is native to Europe

Cautions
Milk thistle based supplements have been measured to have the highest mycotoxin concentrations of up to 37 mg/kg when compared to various plant-based dietary supplements.

Other Information
The plant is sometimes also used as a decorative element in gardens, and its dried flower heads may be used for the decoration of dry bouquets.

Milk Thistle

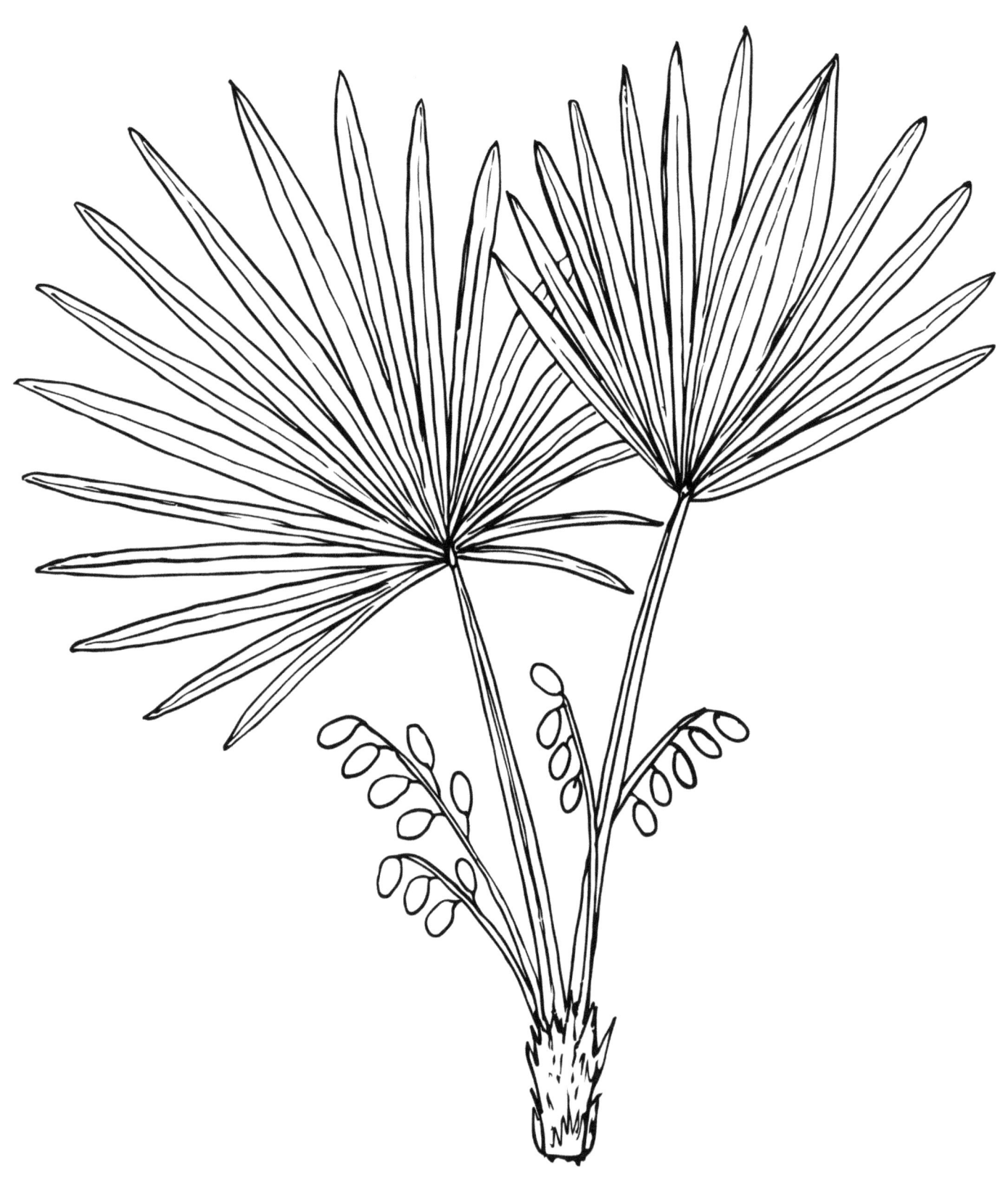

Saw Palmetto
Serenoa repens

Important Facts

- Used to treat Benign Prostatic Hyperplasia (BPH) and its symptoms
- Also used to treat male pattern baldness by reducing the body's levels of dihydrotestosterone (DHT)
- Grows to a maximum height around 7-10 ft

Common Names

Sabal palm, palmetto berry, sabal fructus, cabbage palm, American dwarf palm tree

Parts Used

Fruit

Habitat

Saw Palmetto grows in the islands of the West Indies and Southeastern United States

Cautions

- Should not be taken by those on any blood thinning medication or planning any type of surgery. Taking this herb may increase the risk of bleeding.

Other Information

The leaves are used for thatching by several indigenous groups, so commonly so that a location in Alachua County, Florida, is named Kanapaha ("palm house").

St. John's Wort
Hypericum perforatum

Important Facts

- Known as Nature's anti-depressant, used to treat depression and anxiety.
- Functions as an SSRI (selective serotonin reuptake inhibitor) which allows more serotonin to stay where it's needed to keep you feeling less depressed and anxious
- Used to help quit smoking
- Possesses antiviral properties and can be used externally to treat wounds.
- Perforate St John's wort is a herbaceous perennial plant with extensive, creeping rhizomes. Its reddish stems are erect and branched in the upper section, and can grow up to 3 ft 3 in high.

Common Names
Johnswort, goat weed, hard hay, amber, klamath weed

Parts Used
Fruit

Habitat
St. John's Wort grows in Europe, The United States and Australia

Cautions
Can exacerbate sunburn in fair skinned people. Discuss use of this herb with a doctor before using. St. John's wort can interact in dangerous, sometimes life-threatening ways with a variety of prescribed medicines.

Other Information
It was thought to have medical properties in classical antiquity and was a standard component of theriacs, from the Mithridate of Aulus Cornelius Celsus' De Medicina (ca. 30 AD) to the Venice treacle of d'Amsterdammer Apotheek in 1686.

St. John's Wort

Valerian Root

Valerian Root
Valerian officinalis

Important Facts

- An ancient remedy for insomnia and a great stress buster.
- Active components in this herb increase the production of gamma amino butyric acid (GABA). The brain needs GABA to get to sleep faster and relax.
- Valerian is considered an invasive species in many jurisdictions including Connecticut, US where it is officially banned[35] and in New Brunswick, Canada where it is listed as a plant of concern.

Common Names

St. George's Herb, Set Well, Vandal Root, Fragrant Valerian, English Valerian, Amantilla

Parts Used

Root

Habitat

Valerian is native to Western Europe, Asia and North America

Cautions

- Should not be taken while pregnant
- Do not give to children.

Other Information

Valerian has been used as a medicinal herb since at least the time of ancient Greece and Rome. Hippocrates described its properties, and Galen later prescribed it as a remedy for insomnia.

Valerian root is a cat attractant in a way similar to catnip.

Enjoy other books by

Current and upcoming titles:

Learn and Color Nature Series
- Medicinal Herbs
- Freshwater Fish
- Garden Plants
- Trees
- Bugs and Insects
- Fossils

Learn and Color Stained Glass Series
- Landscapes & Seascapes
- Fish & Fowl
- Flowers
- Birds, Bees, & Butterflies
- Animals
- Designs
- Sea Creatures
- Christian Images

Learn and Color the Bible Series
- Promises
- Prayers
- Proverbs
- Places
- Psalms
- People

Learn and Color Historical Figures Series
- Early Civilization
- The Ancient World
- The Middle Ages
- The Renaissance and Reformation
- The Industrial Revolution
- The Modern Age
- The Present Day

Learn and Color Historical Events Series
- Early Civilization
- The Ancient World
- The Middle Ages
- The Renaissance and Reformation
- The Industrial Revolution
- The Modern Age
- The Present Day

Learn and Color Historical Places Series
- Early Civilization & The Ancient World
- The Middle Ages, Renaissance, & Reformation
- The Modern Age

www.ingramcontent.com/pod-product-compliance
Lightning Source LLC
Chambersburg PA
CBHW051348110526
44591CB00025B/2946